FIGHTING TO SURVIVE BEING LOST AT SEA
TERRIFYING TRUE STORIES

By Elizabeth Raum

COMPASS POINT BOOKS
a capstone imprint

Compass Point Books are published by Capstone Press
1710 Roe Crest Drive, North Mankato, Minnesota 56003
www.capstonepub.com

Library of Congress Cataloging-in-Publication Data
Names: Raum, Elizabeth author.
Title: Fighting to survive being lost at sea : terrifying true stories / by
   Elizabeth Raum.
Description: North Mankato, Minnesota : Capstone Press, [2019] | Series:
   Compass Point Books. Fighting to survive | Audience: Ages: 10-14. |
   Includes bibliographical references and index. | Audience: Age 10-14.
Identifiers: LCCN 2019005974| ISBN 9780756561857 (hardcover) | ISBN
   9780756562328 (paperback) ISBN 9780756562076 (eBook PDF)
Subjects: LCSH: Survival at sea—Juvenile literature. | Marine
   accidents—Juvenile literature. | Shipwreck survival—Juvenile literature.
Classification: LCC G525 .R348 2019 | DDC 910.4/52—dc23
LC record available at https://lccn.loc.gov/2019005974

Editorial Credits
Kristen Mohn, editor; Terri Poburka, designer; Morgan Walters, media researcher;
Kathy McColley, production specialist

Photo Credits
Alamy: G.I.Dobner, 27, World History Archive, 7; Corinne Digges, 45; Getty
Images: Al Seib, 49, Gallo Images, 47, 52, John Lund, Cover, Paul Sutherland, 37,
UniversalImagesGroup, 15; iStockphoto: jcrosemann, 43; Matt Lewis, 39; Newscom: akg-
images, 18, BOURCHIS-TAAF/SIPA/SIPA, 58, Morgan Petroski/ZUMA Press, 9, Splash,
57, World History Archive, 12; Shutterstock: Anton_Ivanov, 51, Bardocz Peter, 4, 54,
DMG Vision, 40, Everett Historical, 10, 17, Inozemtseva_Anna, 33, Isaac Marzioli, (ink)
design element throughout, Miloje, (paper) design element, Natalia Sokko, 25, QArts,
28, ugljesa, 35, Willyam Bradberry, 31, xpixel, (grunge) design element throughout;
Wikimedia: National Geographic Magazine, 20, National Museum of the U.S. Navy, 23

Printed and bound in the USA.
PA71

TABLE OF CONTENTS

INTRODUCTION

The ocean covers almost 71 percent of Earth, but we have only explored about 5 percent of it. We know more about the moon than we do about the ocean, and maps of Mars are more complete than maps of the ocean floor. For example, 12 people have been to the moon, which is nearly 239,000 miles (385,000 kilometers) away. Only three have explored the Mariana Trench in the Pacific basin. At nearly 7 miles (11 km) below the surface of Earth, it is the deepest part of the ocean floor.

The vast ocean is full of sea life—and sunken boats and treasure. There are more artifacts on the ocean floor than in all the museums of the world.

The ocean contains mountain ranges, volcanoes, sunken islands, underwater lakes, rivers, and waterfalls. There are thousands of little-known creatures such as the 8-foot- (2.4-meter-) tall tube worm. Ninety-four percent of the life on Earth is aquatic. Scientists estimate that 86 percent of the species that exist on Earth—many in the ocean—haven't even been discovered by humans.

Despite the many mysteries, or maybe because of them, humans seem drawn to the ocean. Ships carry cargo across the sea, and fishing boats travel vast distances in search of a good catch. For centuries, travelers had to cross the ocean by boat to get from one port to another. Today many people continue to travel on cruise ships, sailboats, or yachts. Some adventurous people seek the challenge of a sea crossing alone or with only a companion or two.

The ocean is not only mysterious—it's also dangerous. Ocean travelers may face massive storms and extreme heat or cold. They may be attacked by powerful sea creatures. Ships and boats break down. At sea, travelers can't simply dial 911 and expect immediate help. They may be thousands of miles from the nearest land.

In the following pages, you'll meet people who have survived shipwrecks, storms, shark attacks, and more. Through courage, wit, and luck, they were able to keep themselves alive until help arrived. These survivors beat the odds.

ICEBERG!
JACK THAYER'S STORY

Before he went to bed the night of April 14, 1912, 17-year-old Jack Thayer stood on the deck of the RMS *Titanic* looking at the stars. "It was the kind of night that made one feel glad to be alive," Jack later said. He had no idea that within a few hours, his life would be put to the test. He was a passenger on the *Titanic's* first and only voyage.

AN EERIE QUIET

Jack was traveling on the British luxury passenger liner with his parents, Marian and John Borland Thayer. The family had been on a tour of Europe and were returning to their home in Haverford, Pennsylvania. They departed from Southampton, England, on April 10, 1912.

On the evening of April 14, Jack ate dinner with his parents in the first-class dining saloon. The 10-course dinner was superb, and the small tables made it easy to join in conversation with those nearby. That evening Jack met 29-year-old Milton Long from Massachusetts. They spent an hour or more talking before saying good night and returning to their cabins.

At 11:40 p.m., as Jack was preparing for bed, he heard a distant thud. He was startled—not by the thud, but by the quiet that followed. Clearly something unusual was happening.

Jack rushed upstairs. At first it was too dark to see much, but his eyes gradually adjusted. He noticed chunks of ice on the deck. The *Titanic* had struck an iceberg!

Jack returned to the stateroom and told his parents what he'd seen. By the time he and his father returned to the deck, the ship wasn't moving. They could feel it listing, or tipping, to one side. Despite the listing, the passengers felt safe. They considered the *Titanic* unsinkable. They didn't know the extent of the damage.

The RMS Titanic *was the largest ship of its time when it set sail on its maiden voyage on April 10, 1912.*

DID YOU KNOW?

Icebergs form on land and float or slide into the ocean. They are common in the north Atlantic Ocean. Scientists think the iceberg the *Titanic* hit formed in Greenland before sliding into the ocean. It towered 100 feet (30 m) above the water and was a few hundred feet long.

CHAOS ON DECK

Back in the stateroom, Jack changed into a heavy green tweed suit. He tied on his life jacket, a bulky canvas vest filled with cork, and put an overcoat on top of it. Jack didn't believe that the ship would sink, but stewards were knocking on doors telling the passengers to put on their life jackets. The Thayers did as instructed before returning to the deck.

The atmosphere of calm curiosity had been replaced with panic as the ship's listing became more severe. Jack's mother was upset, as were many passengers. As Jack later said, "Men and women were running in every direction. Everyone was excited."

The ship's officers ordered the women and children to gather on the port side of the ship and prepare to board the lifeboats. Jack and his father said goodbye to Mrs. Thayer and reported to the starboard side with the men. Jack said, that at the time, "We had no idea the boat would sink."

Jack and Mr. Thayer spoke with Thomas Andrews, the chief engineer. He told them that the ship would not last more than an hour. They were shocked to learn that the unsinkable ship was really going down.

Mr. Thayer learned from a steward that Mrs. Thayer had not yet boarded a lifeboat. Jack and his father found her, and they left together in search of a lifeboat. Along the way Jack found Milton Long, but in the chaos of the crowded deck, he lost sight of his parents.

He hoped his parents had escaped the sinking ship on one of the lifeboats. But Jack would never see his father again.

UNSINKABLE

The ship was going down, but few passengers were aware of the next problem they would face. There weren't enough lifeboats for everyone. The *Titanic* carried slightly more than 2,200 people but had only 16 lifeboats—room for about 1,100 people.

Passengers were initially told that women and children would go first. However, several women refused to enter the lifeboats. Stewards had previously assured them that the *Titanic* could not sink, and the passengers likely believed that boarding the lifeboats would be more dangerous than staying on the damaged ship. Many waited until it was too late.

John "Jack" Thayer V keeps a picture on his phone of his grandfather, John "Jack" Thayer III, who survived the Titanic *disaster.*

German artist Willy Stower's 1912 painting, Sinking of the Titanic

DECISION TIME

Jack and Milton pushed their way through the crowd to the starboard side. Two lifeboats remained, but so many people crowded around it that Jack and Milton didn't even try to board.

Time was running out. By now, it was obvious to most people that the *Titanic* was sinking, but Jack wasn't one to give up hope. As the *Titanic* tilted further into the water, people began jumping into the sea, believing that the lifeboats would rescue them.

Three times Jack planned to jump. Three times Milton told him to wait, hoping that some other solution would present itself. Jack said later, "Even then we thought she might possibly stay afloat."

The boat tipped further and sank deeper into the ocean. People slid and fell as the angle of the deck became even steeper.

Jack later wrote, "We were a mass of hopeless, dazed humanity, attempting, as the Almighty and Nature made us, to keep our final breath until the last possible moment."

Jack and Milton were now only about 12 to 15 feet (4 to 5 m) above the water. They decided it was now or never. They shook hands and climbed onto the ship's railing. Milton dangled his legs over the edge and asked Jack if he was coming.

"In a minute," Jack said, gathering his courage.

Milton jumped. He slid down the side of the ship and disappeared from sight. Just a few hours after they had met, they had already said their final goodbye. Jack never saw his friend again.

Seconds later, Jack also leapt feet first into the ocean. He jumped clear of the ship and slid beneath the water. He struggled to reach the surface.

Those few seconds of delay may have saved Jack's life. When he emerged, he realized that he'd been pushed some distance away from the ship, rather than being pulled underneath the ship as he had feared. From the water, he watched as the ship broke in two.

DID YOU KNOW?

Each lifeboat was designed to hold 65 people, but many were launched just half full. Officials later said they feared that full lifeboats would break apart when lowered into the water. Sadly, only two lifeboats attempted to rescue stranded passengers.

AN UNFORGETTABLE SIGHT

The force of the breaking ship sucked Jack underwater. He fought his way to the surface again and came up amid scattered wreckage. He saw several men sitting atop an overturned lifeboat nearby. One of them reached out and helped Jack climb on. He joined the men huddled together on the overturned boat. They stayed as still as they could to avoid falling off their precarious perch. In all, 25 men had scrambled onto the boat.

Passengers from the Titanic *waited in their lifeboat for rescue from the* Carpathia.

Jack faced the *Titanic*. Both pieces of the ship tipped at a 60-degree angle into the sea and hung there for a moment. Then, with a huge hissing sound, they plunged beneath the water. There was nothing left of the unsinkable ship. It had stayed afloat only two hours and 40 minutes after hitting the iceberg.

Jack and the others on the overturned lifeboat worried that the force of the sinking ship would suck them under the sea. The suction did pull the lifeboat closer to the spot where the *Titanic* had been, but not with as much strength as expected. Jack and the others managed to stay afloat. People struggled to swim through the icy waters nearby, but there was nothing Jack could do to help them. There was no more room atop the crowded lifeboat.

After the *Titanic* disappeared below the surface, the waters became calm again. Stars still shone in the sky. Waves lapped at the boat. The men prayed and sang hymns as they waited for dawn.

A BIT OF HOPE

The *Titanic*'s wireless operator was among the group on Jack's boat. Before he jumped overboard, he'd received a message from another British passenger liner, the *Carpathia*. He told the other men it was on its way. The news gave Jack hope. None of them would survive much longer in the freezing, wet cold.

The *Carpathia* had received the *Titanic*'s distress call at 12:20 a.m. on April 15. Despite the presence of icebergs, Captain Arthur Rostron traveled the 58 miles (93 km) to the *Titanic*'s position at top speed. The ship arrived an hour and a half after the *Titanic* sank.

RESCUE

The men on Jack's boat spotted the *Carpathia*'s light. Rescue seemed possible, but getting from the unstable, overturned lifeboat onto the *Carpathia* presented yet another danger.

Other *Titanic* lifeboats filled with women and children became visible nearby. One of the men in Jack's group had a whistle. He blew it, and, slowly, lifeboats #4 and #12 rowed their way toward them. Now that the *Titanic* had sunk, people manning the lifeboats felt safer trying to rescue others needing help. It took them more than an hour to reach the men who were perilously balanced on the overturned boat. Each lifeboat had room for about half the men. All 25 found a place in the more stable lifeboats.

Jack climbed into lifeboat #12. He never noticed his mother handling one of the oars on lifeboat #4. She didn't see him either. About 45 minutes later, the *Carpathia* pulled alongside the lifeboats and began bringing the survivors on board.

REUNION

It wasn't until about 8:30 that morning that Jack found his mother on the *Carpathia*. She immediately asked about her husband, but Jack had no idea where his father might be. They learned later that Mr. Thayer was among the more than 1,500 passengers who went down with the ship or died in the freezing waters.

Three days after the *Titanic* sank, the *Carpathia* reached New York. Jack and his mother took a train home to Pennsylvania. Jack completed high school, graduating in the spring. The next fall he enrolled at the University of Pennsylvania. He became a banker like his father had been. Eventually, he returned to the University of Pennsylvania as the financial vice president and treasurer. He married and had five children.

Rescued passengers recovered on the deck of the Carpathia, *which saved about 705 people from the* Titanic.

Jack rarely spoke about the *Titanic* disaster until his own children became teenagers. At that time he wrote a brief account of his survival, titled "The Sinking of the S.S. *Titanic*." Jack died in 1945 at age 50.

TORPEDOES!
POON LIM'S STORY

In 1941, 23-year-old Poon Lim took a job as second mess steward on the British merchant ship SS *Ben Lomond*. At the time, many of the world's countries were fighting World War II (1939–1945). Poon Lim was Chinese, and Japanese troops were preparing to attack China and Hong Kong. Serving meals in the ship's dining hall and performing housekeeping duties seemed far safer than fighting the war on land. However, as it turned out, Poon Lim fought as hard as any soldier. His enemy was the sea.

ATTACK

China and Japan weren't the only nations at war. German U-boats were prowling the seas for British ships. Even so, Poon Lim's first few months on *Ben Lomond* passed without incident.

Ben Lomond left Cape Town, South Africa, on November 10, 1942, for South America. It would then continue to New York. The big merchant ship traveled slowly, far from other friendly ships. By November 23, *Ben Lomond* was in the Atlantic Ocean about 750 miles (1,200 km) east of Brazil's Amazon River.

Just before noon that day, a German U-boat spotted *Ben Lomond* and launched two torpedoes. Both made direct hits. *Ben Lomond* was sinking fast. Poon Lim grabbed a life jacket and jumped overboard.

Poon Lim's life jacket kept him afloat as the ship's boilers exploded and the ship disappeared into the sea. The 6,630-ton ship sank less than two minutes after the attack.

ALONE

Poon Lim searched for other survivors. More than 50 men served on the ship, but Poon Lim didn't see a single one. Had no one else survived? Poon Lim tried not to panic as he bobbed up and down with the waves. The life jacket was literally a lifesaver, as he had never learned to swim.

After about two hours, Poon Lim spotted an empty wooden raft with a canvas cover and a small sail. He paddled toward the raft and managed to climb aboard. Someone else from *Ben Lomond* had apparently launched it but never used it. Poon Lim didn't want to think about what had happened to that sailor or his other crewmates. He was simply relieved to get out of the water. At least for a moment or two, he felt safe.

German artist Adolf Bock's 1941 painting shows German sailors on the tower of a U-boat after torpedoing a British cargo ship.

THE RAFT

Once he was settled on the raft and somewhat calmer, Poon Lim checked for supplies. He found two cans of dried crackers, about 2 quarts (1.8 liters) of water, some milk, a bag of sugar cubes, chocolate, a small electric stove, a flashlight, and a few flares. Of course, he still had the life jacket and the clothes he was wearing. He worried about falling overboard, so he tied a rope to his wrist. If he fell, he could use it to pull himself back to the raft.

Poon Lim waited for rescue. Because the attack had come without warning and the ship had sunk so quickly, it seemed

A British merchant vessel went down in the Atlantic after a German submarine hit it with a torpedo during World War II.

unlikely that anyone had time to call for help. Still, Poon Lim could hope. He had no idea how long it might be before someone would come to his rescue, but he was determined to survive.

SURVIVING

As the days passed, Poon Lim realized that he would have to be clever to survive at sea. He rationed his food supply to make it last, but the water wouldn't last long. He couldn't drink seawater—that would dehydrate him faster than no water at all. He needed to find drinkable water. He used the canvas from his life jacket and the raft's canopy to catch rainwater. It didn't take long for Poon Lim's food supplies to run out either. The ocean was full of fish, but he didn't have any fishing gear.

Poon Lim dug a nail out of the raft's wood and shaped it into a hook. He cut some rope from the sail to use as a fishing line. He fashioned a knife out of one of the empty cracker cans. Later, after the flashlight battery died, he made another fish hook from one of the springs inside it. For bait, he crushed crackers and rolled them in water to form a paste. At first he caught small fish, which he used as bait to catch bigger ones. He ate the fish raw.

DID YOU KNOW?

Although small amounts of salt are healthy, the amount of salt in seawater can overpower the kidneys. The kidneys need fresh water to make urine and eliminate extra salt. Drinking seawater causes dehydration. Over time, it is fatal.

PASSING BY

Poon Lim made knots in a rope to count the passing days, but after several weeks at sea, he gave up counting days. Instead, he counted the full moons. Months passed. So did ships, but they didn't stop. At first, Poon Lim believed they didn't stop because he was Chinese. Later, he realized that they simply didn't see him. He was a tiny speck in a huge ocean. The dingy white canvas of

Poon Lim on his raft

his sail probably looked like just another whitecap to passing ships. A German U-boat spotted Poon Lim but left him alone. A U.S. Navy plane passed overhead. The pilot dropped a dye marker into the sea so that a rescue ship could find him, but a storm washed away the marker before the ship reached him. Each hope of rescue was dashed.

STORM

Poon Lim spent his days fishing. He didn't stop even when he had enough to eat. He laid the fish out in the sun and dried them for later, creating a good supply of food.

Then a huge storm hit. Waves rocked the raft, and water poured inside of it. Poon Lim held on, but his supply of fish and drinking water were washed overboard. Weak and devastated, he knew he would only survive a few days without water.

Poon Lim had to find something to drink. He watched the birds that often flew around his raft. When one landed nearby, he reached out and caught it. Desperate for liquid, he cut it open and drank its blood. Revived, he caught several more birds. Drinking their blood kept him alive until the rains came again.

As the months wore on, Poon Lim suffered from sunburn and seasickness. He developed painful sores on his body, both from the salt water and the unrelenting sun. Powerful storms tossed his raft on the waves. Worse yet, sharks began to circle. The remains of the birds and fish that Poon Lim tossed into the sea attracted the sharks. They scared off the smaller fish, his only source of food. If he wanted to eat, Poon Lim would have to catch a shark.

CATCHING A SHARK

Poon Lim had some bird meat for bait. He then took the canvas from his life jacket to make protective coverings for his hands. He used the bait to lure a small shark toward him. When the shark took the bait, he hauled the thrashing creature onto the raft. The shark fought. It bit Poon Lim, but he fought back. Even though he was bleeding, in pain, weak, and hungry, he wrestled the shark in a life-or-death battle.

Finally, Poon Lim bashed in the shark's head with a half-filled water bottle. He was so thirsty that he cut into its liver and drank the blood. Then he ate the meat. Next he cut off the shark fins and dried them in the sun. Shark fin, a delicacy in China, gave Poon Lim a taste of home.

RESCUE

After more than four months at sea, Poon Lim noticed the water changing color. He had floated near land! On April 5, 1943, three Brazilian fishermen found him in a bay off the coast of Brazil.

British authorities in Brazil, amazed that he had survived so long, posed for pictures with him before taking him to the hospital. Poon Lim had lost 20 pounds (9 kilograms). He spent four weeks in the hospital and made a full recovery.

Great Britain's Royal Navy incorporated Poon Lim's story into its survival manuals so that others could learn from his experience. In October 1943, Great Britain's King George VI awarded Poon Lim the British Empire Medal for service worthy of recognition by the Crown. Poon Lim had survived for 133 days on a small wooden raft, despite the fact that he couldn't swim. In doing so, he set a world record. When he was asked about being the record holder he said, "I hope no one will ever have to break that record."

Poon Lim explained to a U.S. Navy rear admiral how he had made a fish hook from the spring in a flashlight.

DID YOU KNOW?

After the war Poon Lim wanted to move the United States, but Chinese people were no longer being allowed into the country at the time. However, Poon Lim's ordeal had made him famous, and he was given special consideration. With the help of U.S. Senator Warren Magnuson from Washington state, Poon Lim was eventually granted U.S. citizenship.

WHALE ATTACK!
WILLIAM AND SIMONNE BUTLER'S STORY

William and Simonne Butler left Miami, Florida, on April 14, 1989, for a four-year, round-the-world cruise in their sailboat, *Siboney*. William was a retired engineer and an expert sailor who had sailed from Miami to Maine in the United States, as well as to Bermuda and Venezuela. This cruise was William's lifelong dream. Simonne, his wife, was less enthusiastic.

The trip started well. The Butlers had smooth sailing as they crossed through the Panama Canal. On May 23 they entered the Pacific Ocean. By June 15, they were 1,200 nautical miles (2,200 km) west-southwest of Panama. They headed to Hawaii, where they planned to stop and enjoy the sights.

The sea was calm. William turned on the automatic pilot. It allowed them to sleep at night without needing a sailor at the helm. They went to their sleeping quarters below deck. A few hours before dawn, a loud thump woke them.

SURROUNDED

William went topside. "We found ourselves surrounded by 20 to 30 whales," he said later. "They were blowing, they were mad. I didn't know what to do. There was 45 minutes of bashing. Then it was over."

He knew immediately that the sailboat was badly damaged. The whale attack had punched a hole in the fiberglass that formed the bottom of the boat. Water was pouring into the boat.

William sent a Mayday message asking other boats in the area to come to the rescue. He and Simonne gathered what supplies they could and scrambled onto the sailboat's emergency life raft. Within 15 minutes of the attack, *Siboney* had sunk.

"We grabbed a lot of things we didn't need," Simonne said later. Things like a gun without ammunition and a video camera without batteries. But they also made some smart decisions. They grabbed a water purifier, some canned food, and a fishing pole—things they would need to survive adrift in the Pacific Ocean.

Boats can harm whales, and whales can cause significant damage to boats.

DID YOU KNOW?

Biologists believe that sperm whales attacked the Butlers' boat. Sperm whales live in all the world's oceans and are the largest of the toothed whales. They weigh between 15 and 45 tons and are up to 59 feet (18 m) long—larger than the Butlers' boat.

THE RAFT

William and Simonne, shaken by the attack, huddled together in the 6-foot (2-m) rubber raft. As the shock wore off, they sorted through their supplies. They had a flashlight, three flares, a hook, and a fishing line. They also found a compass, a knife, and two blankets, which would help them stay warm at night.

Their supplies included nine cans of food, half a jar of peanut butter, two cans of crackers, and two jugs of water. The water purifier would make salt water drinkable. Unsure of how long they would be stranded, the Butlers knew they would have to ration their food supply. They ate sparingly.

GAMES

William said, "The first two weeks we would play dominoes in the morning so we could keep our minds off what was actually happening to us. We would play '20 Questions' and other mind games." It helped to pass the days, which seemed to stretch on forever.

Soon, though, they had to stop playing and focus on survival. Dolphins and sea turtles kept bumping into the raft, poking holes in it. William and Simonne plugged the holes with a small patch kit they found on the raft. It became an endless task.

At night sharks surrounded the raft. They were attracted to the small fish that found shelter beneath it. The Butlers couldn't scare off the small fish, so they kicked the sharks away. But the sharks returned during the night and poked holes in the raft, causing leaks. William and Simonne bailed out the water until daylight, when they could see the holes and repair them.

A life raft similar to the one the Butlers used after their sailboat sank

The sun beat down relentlessly. Even with the raft's canopy, the Butlers had painful sunburns. Food was running low, and with no rescue in sight, Simonne began to lose hope and feel depressed. William struggled to keep up her spirits. He feared that if she gave up, they wouldn't survive. He reminded her that she had loved ones at home who needed her. "Our family was our reason to survive," he said. They prayed for rescue.

FOOD

Despite rationing, the Butlers ran out of food in about a month. William had been dragging the fishing line and hook, but he hadn't caught anything. One day a huge turtle swam by. William grabbed it. They ate some of the meat immediately and saved the rest as bait. William used the bait to catch triggerfish.

William ate his fill of fish, but Simonne hated it. She said it was too chewy, so William cut the fish into tiny pieces and told her to imagine she was eating chicken. She managed to eat some, but even so, she kept losing weight.

DANGERS

In addition to attacks by sharks, turtles, and dolphins damaging the raft, storms and waves tossed and battered it. William and Simonne's clothes turned to rags, and their skin developed sores from the constant exposure to salt water and intense sun. Simonne became dizzy, so William encouraged her to eat more.

One night they heard a scraping sound, which was probably caused by a dolphin. Its dorsal fin sliced into the raft, and water gushed in. "We're sinking!" Simonne yelled.

They took turns bailing water throughout the night. The next morning, they found the slit in the raft. A patch wouldn't do, but Simonne had a small toiletry bag with a needle and thread. She and William sewed the slit closed with 11 stitches. Even so, water continued to slowly leak into the raft. They didn't have to bail constantly, but their situation steadily became more desperate. The raft barely floated. If help didn't come soon, the Butlers would have no choice but to swim with the sharks. They knew that would be the end.

Several species of sea turtles live in the Pacific Ocean where the Butlers were stranded.

RESCUE?

While the Butlers drifted at sea, they spotted more than 40 boats. Even though they screamed for help, not one of the boats noticed them. They were just a small speck on a huge ocean. They had drifted 900 miles (1,400 km) from where *Siboney* went down. They didn't have a two-way radio, but they had a small music player that picked up a few radio stations. The radio gave them hints about their location as they drifted, picking up stations from Los Angeles, Texas, Guatemala, Costa Rica, and Panama.

On Friday, August 18, 1989, they saw a merchant ship in the distance. William fired his last flare. The Butlers thought that the ship had seen them, but it didn't stop. It sailed on.

Now even William was about to give up hope.

Then, the very next day, August 19, they heard a loud engine. "We were so overjoyed we started crying and hugging," Simonne said.

A Costa Rican Coast Guard vessel steamed toward them. They were just 13 miles (21 km) off the Costa Rican coast when they were rescued. They'd been adrift for 66 days. The Coast Guard took them to a hospital in Golfito, Costa Rica, to recover. As soon as they were able, they flew home to Miami.

William planned to return to sailing within a year. Simonne felt differently. "I like being on land, solid ground," she said. "I like green trees and flowers, no more blue for a while."

In 2005 William wrote a book about their ordeal, called *66 Days Adrift: A True Story of Disaster and Survival on the Open Sea*. He has never stopped sailing.

Sperm whales swim in pods. A single whale can be larger than a school bus.

DID YOU KNOW?

Dr. Lindy Weilgart, a Canadian researcher, says, "I do believe a sperm whale is capable of the aggression necessary to attack a ship, especially a mother if her young was threatened." Constance Gavin of the New England Aquarium believes it's possible that the whales saw the Butlers' boat as another animal "or one of their own." She added, "Whales will bump and bash a lot among themselves and, while it wouldn't hurt a whale, it could certainly hurt a little boat."

FLOODED!
MATT LEWIS'S STORY

When Matt Lewis accepted a job as scientific observer on a South African fishing boat, he had no idea he was putting his life in danger. He'd just finished his degree in zoology from the University of Aberdeen in Scotland. He wanted to be a marine biologist, and the job on the fishing boat seemed like a good start. He flew to Cape Town, South Africa, in April 1998 to begin work.

Lewis expected to see a well-equipped, modern fishing boat. However, *Sudur Havid* was not only smaller than the other boats in port, but its bow was dented and its stern was rusty. The 34-year-old boat had been altered over the years to meet the needs of the different fishing crews it carried. Now it was headed to the Antarctic seas to catch Patagonian toothfish.

Lewis realized that quarters would be tight. The crew of 38 men included members of South Africa's Xhosa tribe and members of Namibia's Ovambo tribe. Few spoke English. Most were fishermen, but they didn't know how to swim. Of the 38 who left the South African port on April 6, 1998, only 21 returned home.

Cape Town, South Africa, is a major fishing and trade port.

WINTER

Winter was coming when *Sudur Havid* sailed into the Southern Ocean, but the waters were fairly calm. Lewis watched the crew fish for toothfish. They tossed baited hooks into the water at night and hauled in the catch each morning. Lewis kept records of the number of fish caught and noted whether any birds were snared. Observers on fishing boats, such as Lewis, were required to make sure the crew obeyed environmental laws.

The sea became rough about two months into the journey. At first Lewis had trouble keeping his balance. When the boat plowed into a swell, it sprayed the deck with water. Lewis had to grab the handrail to stay upright. Gradually he adjusted to the constant rocking from wind and waves.

On June 6 conditions grew far more dangerous. Winter had arrived. The water temperature was below freezing, the wind roared, and waves reached 33 feet (10 m) in height—taller than a three-story house. Lewis could barely stand upright, but the storm didn't keep the fishermen from working.

DID YOU KNOW?

In the Southern Hemisphere, the seasons are opposite those in the Northern Hemisphere, where North America is located. In the Southern Hemisphere, where the Southern Ocean, also called the Antarctic Ocean, is located, summer begins in December. Winter begins in June.

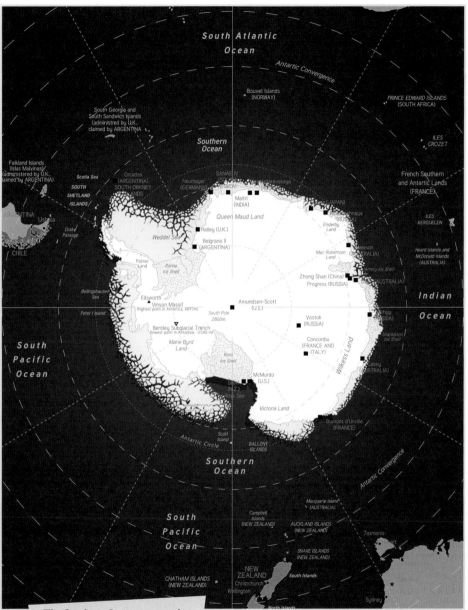

The Southern Ocean surrounds
Antarctica and is home to several
species of deepwater fish.

Icy water surged into the factory area of the boat where the fishermen cleaned the fish and prepared them for storage. Normally, pumps drained the water back into the sea, but the pumps stopped working. Worse yet, no one knew how to fix them. The water in the boat got deeper and deeper. Lewis and the others stood knee-deep in frigid water that kept rolling in. The boat began to list to one side. Where was the engineer who could fix the pumps? Lewis rushed to find him.

He found the ship's electrician drinking coffee in the crew dining room and told him that they desperately needed help with the diesel pump.

The man said he wasn't on duty.

DID YOU KNOW?

The giant Patagonian toothfish dwells in cold, deep ocean waters. It lives up to 60 years and has a mouth full of razor-sharp teeth. It may reach 7 feet (2 m) in length and weigh up to 220 pounds (100 kg). In restaurants it's often called Chilean sea bass.

An Indonesian fisherman with his Patagonian toothfish catch

BROKEN PUMPS

Lewis dragged the electrician into the factory and ordered him to fix the pump. The electrician took one look at the pump and said he didn't know how to fix it, but that the chief engineer might.

Lewis found the chief engineer asleep in his bunk. After several minutes of trying to attach a new cable to the fuse box, the engineer shook his head. He finally came up with a solution but said that it would take an hour. Lewis knew they didn't have an hour. The boat was already sinking.

Lewis told the skipper that it was time to quit fishing. The situation seemed obvious, but the skipper brushed aside the warnings. So did the fishing master. Both men disregarded the danger despite the reports from the factory floor.

The lights in the factory area went out. A huge wave slammed into the boat, and Lewis heard what sounded like a gunshot as the storm door burst open. He peered into the darkness and saw water reaching nearly to the ceiling on one side of the tilting boat. With no time to waste, he plunged into waist-deep water and made his way to the stairs leading to the upper deck.

LIFE RAFTS

When Lewis reached the deck, he was shocked to discover that the boat didn't even have cold-water survival suits. These suits are designed to help a person withstand extremely cold conditions. Even a healthy person can't last longer than 45 minutes in the freezing ocean water. It was then that he remembered his first sight of the boat and his dismay at its condition. He had been right to be concerned.

Lewis was even more upset to see the senior crew members and the engineer packing their belongings. They hadn't put out a call to the rest of the crew to abandon ship. They also had not sent out

Built in the early 1960s, Sudur Havid *was in poor condition before the incident.*

an SOS message or set up emergency beacons that would notify other ships of their distress. Two of the men jumped into a life raft and left without a word of instruction to the crew. They floated away—two men in a raft designed to hold 20.

JUMPING SHIP

"What's happening?" Lewis asked. "Are we abandoning ship or what?"

"Yes," a deckhand said as he scrambled into a life jacket.

Lewis hurried to his cabin to put on a flotation suit. He fumbled with the suit, unable to zip it up fully. He didn't know if it would still protect him, but it was the best option he had.

Wind conditions in the Southern Ocean have generated some of the largest waves ever recorded.

When Lewis returned to the deck, he helped the crew toss the two large canisters holding the two remaining life rafts overboard. When they hit the water, the canisters burst open, releasing the inflatable rafts. At least there would be enough room for everyone. Deckhands tied the rafts to the boat's railing so they wouldn't float away as the men climbed inside. But the waves tossed the rafts up and down, crashing them into the ship. Boarding wouldn't be easy.

Several of the deckhands didn't even know how to fasten their life jackets, so Lewis helped them. All the while he kept hoping that another boat would come to their rescue. He didn't want to board a life raft until everyone else was off the ship, but he knew he couldn't wait long. In only two hours, it would be dark. Darkness would make everything more difficult.

NO OTHER OPTIONS

The storm raged on, and *Sudur Havid* sank deeper into the churning waters. Soon, there was no choice but to board the rafts. Lewis tried to reassure the men, and it seemed to help. No one screamed or panicked. But they would have to jump from the bobbing ship to make it. If they were lucky, they would jump directly through the narrow opening in the canopies on the rafts. If not, they would land in the water and have to swim and climb into the raft. For the many who couldn't swim, it was a horrifying thought. They hesitated, wasting precious moments.

"Just jump, man, just jump!" Lewis yelled.

LAST MAN OFF

Eugene, a deckhand, leapt into the air, missed the smaller raft, and disappeared beneath the water. He surfaced and attempted to swim to the bigger raft, even though it was farther away. Several other men who had missed the narrow canopy opening were already in the water, struggling to swim.

The two rafts filled with sailors. Several men still bobbed in the water, trying to stay afloat and reach a raft. Many disappeared beneath the churning sea.

Lewis knew it was time for him to abandon ship, but he felt that he couldn't leave while others were still aboard. The second raft had already left. Lewis searched and was surprised to find the fishing master, staggering onto the deck.

"Come on!" Lewis urged.

But the fishing master refused. He insisted on saving the skipper, who had collapsed on the deck. The skipper's skin was ash-gray.

Lewis helped the skipper up onto the rail. As the raft rose on the waves, Lewis pushed him over the rail into the remaining raft. He landed safely, but it was obvious that he was seriously ill.

Now Lewis was the only man left. He tensed, waiting for the raft to rise up on the swell of the wave. When it did, he jumped.

"I wasn't scared," he wrote later. "I was exhilarated. Whatever was going to happen, at least we were off the sinking ship. I was the last man off."

But the raft was still tied to *Sudur Havid*. Waves tossed it back and forth. When the fishing boat sank, the raft and its occupants would go down with it. The men needed a knife to cut the raft free, but no one had one.

CUTTING FREE

Sudur Havid's bow was now underwater. The boat's stern rose into the air, pulling the raft up with it. As it was lifted into the air, the raft banged into the fishing boat's metal hull. Lewis's head hit the side of the ship.

Somehow the raft finally pulled free of the ship, but then it began to flood. Although the raft was now filled with freezing water, at least the men were detached from *Sudur Havid*. And it was just in time.

DRIFTING ALONE

With a final shudder, *Sudur Havid* sank. The steady rumble of its engines stopped. The men were drifting alone in a vast sea 170 miles (274 km) from the nearest island. There was no sign of the other two rafts. Lewis and his companions found a crew member swimming and pulled him into the raft, bringing the total to 17 in a raft built for 12. Survival time would be short—the men were up to their waists in icy water.

Lewis checked the raft for supplies. He found no paddles or buckets to bail out the water or any flares to attract a rescue ship.

The raft should have had a light atop it, but it didn't.

Lewis tried to close the raft's doors, but his hands were already stiff with cold. Every time he sealed the door, the wind blew it open, and more water sprayed inside. Hypothermia, injuries, and stress were already taking a toll. Some men groaned, while others wailed. Still others were deadly quiet.

When Lewis glanced outside, he spied one of the other rafts. It had a working light on top. The men tried to paddle toward it with their hands, but they got nowhere.

Lewis and 16 other men crammed into a life raft built for 12.

ISLA CAMILA

As they floated in the battered raft, their bodies grew more chilled by the minute. Lewis's legs were numb, and his fingers stopped working. No one had enough energy to speak. They'd been in the raft for three long hours when it began to sink.

Unknown to Lewis, before *Sudur Havid* sank, the skipper had managed to send a distress signal, which included the boat's location. The nearest boat was *Isla Camila*, a Spanish fishing boat. Captain Ernesto Sandoval Agurto responded to the call, but it took *Isla Camila* three hours to travel 33 miles (53 km) through the storm to reach the survivors. When *Isla Camila* arrived at the site of the sinking, it found nothing.

The officers sent flares. No one responded.

The ship slowed and searched the water for 30 minutes before a deckhand spotted the flashing light atop one of the life rafts. The ship moved toward it to recover survivors.

That was when Lewis spotted *Isla Camila* from his raft.

"There's a light!" Lewis exclaimed. "Come on, guys, there's a boat! We need to yell!" He knew that without a light on their raft, yelling was their only chance of attracting the rescue ship's attention.

And yell they did.

RESCUE

The *Isla Camila* crew heard them, moved in, and began to rescue the men in Lewis's raft. It was a slow and difficult process. They were horrified to discover that several of the men in the raft were already dead, including the skipper.

After the disaster, a South African review board blamed the

Matt Lewis hiking in Scotland

ship's officers for causing the loss of 17 lives. If the skipper and fishing master had listened to Lewis and the deckhands and stopped fishing earlier, the crew could have closed the factory doors sooner. That would have stopped the flooding and allowed them to repair the pumps before the ship was overwhelmed.

Eventually Lewis returned to Scotland. He married and had two children. He wrote a book, called *Last Man Off*, about his experience, and he now spends most of his time on land teaching children about the environment. He swims in the rivers near his home but has no plans to return to the Southern Ocean.

WINDS!
ABBY SUNDERLAND'S STORY

Thirteen-year-old Abby Sunderland dreamed of sailing around the world alone. She'd spent her life around sailboats. Beginning when Abby was 8, her family spent three years living on a sailboat. They cruised from port to port. By the time she was 13, Abby was delivering 30-foot (10-m) sailboats up and down the California coast for her dad, who owned a yacht company.

Abby loved sailing. "For me, a day on the water was every bit as normal as a day ashore," she said. She had never been on the water alone for a long period of time, but she dreamed of taking a solo sailing trip around the world. A trip that long—22,000 miles (35,000 km)—would take six months or longer. Abby would be on her own—far from home, far from anyone. Her parents said she could go when she turned 16.

PREPARATIONS

In 2008 and 2009 Abby's 17-year-old brother Zac completed a solo round-the-world sailing trip. Once Zac was home safe, Abby's parents helped her prepare for her trip.

Abby and her dad flew to Rhode Island to purchase a 40-foot (12-m) sailboat. Abby named it *Wild Eyes*. A team of sailing experts replaced the rigging, overhauled the engine, and outfitted the boat with extra batteries and automatic pilots. They set up an internet connection so Abby could receive weather reports and stay in touch with family and friends by email.

A company called Shoe City agreed to sponsor Abby, which helped fund the expensive trip. Later, when repair costs increased, she gained three more sponsors.

Abby took trial runs up and down the California coast. She also met with a dietitian to plan healthy meals. She would eat dehydrated food packed in watertight bags during the months at sea.

CRITICS

Many people thought the trip was too dangerous for a 16-year-old. Their comments were so harsh that Abby began to doubt herself. When she realized that it was impossible to please everyone, and she began to feel more confident. She ignored the critics and focused on training and preparing for the trip.

Abby hoped to become the youngest person to sail solo, nonstop, around the world.

SETTING SAIL

Abby left Marina Del Rey, California, on January 23, 2010. Family and friends stood on the dock and waved goodbye.

Abby spent her first days at sea learning when to eat, when to sleep, and how to keep the boat clean and orderly. She loved seeing dolphins, watching sunsets, and sailing with the wind. Using wi-fi via satellite, she was able to stay connected to her family and friends and feel less alone at sea. She answered emails and wrote a blog.

STARTING OVER

Unfortunately, in those first few days, Abby learned that the solar panels and wind generators on *Wild Eyes* weren't creating enough power to keep the boat sailing in calm seas. She decided to at Cabo San Lucas, Mexico, to get more fuel to power the boat on windless days. She called her support team, who agreed with the decision.

Abby wanted to make the trip nonstop, so she decided to start her trip again from Cabo San Lucas. She planned to end it there as well.

Abby reached Cabo on February 2. Her dad and several supporters were there to meet her. After more than a week on the boat, Abby had trouble walking on land. She wobbled up the dock.

She spent the next few days refitting the boat. It felt good to see her dad, eat fresh food, and enjoy time with those who gathered to wish her well. On February 6 Abby sailed away into strong winds and massive sea swells. "Some days," she reported, "a dense, soupy fog dropped over the boat . . . it was like sailing inside a grey envelope."

Abby adjusted the rigging of Wild Eyes *as she prepared for her trip.*

As Abby neared the equator, the weather became hotter and hotter, and the air was humid and rainy. She wore a swimsuit and poured salt water over her head to stay cool. On February 19 she crossed the equator. Sailors celebrate that milestone with a special ceremony. Abby videotaped the moment and poured more salt water over her head. She then sailed south along the coast of South America and into the Southern Ocean, leaving the equatorial heat behind.

TIME TO QUIT?

Cape Horn, at the southernmost point of South America, is a dangerous place for sailors because of its strong winds. Cold, wet gusts roared around Abby, leaving her soaking wet and shivering.

At this point, the autopilots on Abby's boat began to fail. She stayed up all night to keep the boat on course. Her hands became numb, and she was soaked and tired. The boat pitched and shifted in the winds, and heavy rain began falling. Without the autopilots, she couldn't leave the helm. Although she could stay awake for one night, eventually she would have to sleep.

She called home for advice. Two experts worked with her through the night. They suggested possible solutions over the phone. As Abby lay in the rain on the wet deck trying first one repair and then another, the boat drifted closer and closer to the islands at the southern tip of Chile. *Wild Eyes* was in danger of crashing into the sharp rocks surrounding the islands.

Abby's team prepared to give up, but Abby didn't. For hours, she tried whatever the experts on the phone suggested. Suddenly, one of the repairs worked! Abby sailed on.

SETTING A RECORD

The next day, March 31, 2010, Abby became the youngest person to sail solo around Cape Horn. Unfortunately, she was so exhausted from a night spent repairing the autopilot that she slept through it.

Wild Eyes sailed toward the Falkland Islands. Strong winds and warm temperatures helped Abby make good time. About 1,500 miles (2,400 km) beyond the Falklands, the winds increased to 58 miles (93 km) per hour. Abby had to lower the mainsail. In high winds it would cause the boat to keel, or lean too far over the water. The boat was in danger of capsizing. The darkness and cold, wet winds made the job of lowering the sail extremely difficult. Abby strapped into a harness and began climbing the rigging. The boat tipped toward the sea, lowering Abby and the rigging so far down that her legs hit the water. Fear surged through her.

The Falkland Islands are about 300 miles (480 km) east of the coast of Argentina.

CRISIS

To reach the sail, Abby had to climb over the boom, which held the sail in position. She couldn't reach it with her safety harness on, so she unclipped the harness that held her to the boat and dropped to the deck. One false move and she would be blown into the ocean at night in high winds and rolling seas. It would be deadly.

She clung to the boat's handrail as waves washed over her. The mast was nearly in the water, but somehow she managed to pull down the sail. The boat steadied. For the moment, at least, she was safe. She continued her journey.

ANOTHER FAILURE

In mid-April, the autopilots stopped working again. This time, Abby decided to stop in Cape Town, South Africa, for repairs.

Abby reached Cape Town on May 5. She had already spent 100 days alone at sea, traveling halfway around the world. *Wild Eyes* needed several repairs, and Abby spent the time with her dad, who had flown from California to see her. They discussed her options about finishing the trip. Abby decided to continue. She wanted to complete her solo journey even if it was no longer nonstop.

After Cape Town, Abby would be crossing the Indian Ocean during the storm season. She knew there would be no other help until she reached Australia, more than 6,000 miles (9,600 km) away.

THE FINAL PUSH

With the repairs made, Abby left Cape Town May 21 and sailed into the Indian Ocean. It's the warmest ocean in the world, but is also prone to intense tropical storms. Sailors consider it one of the most dangerous oceans.

Abby sailed into rough weather. In late May the lines of her sail became tangled, causing her concern, but the lines untangled, and she kept sailing. A few days later, she hit even stronger winds. Waves rushed into the boat, soaking her engine. She pumped out the water and continued on her way.

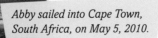

Abby sailed into Cape Town, South Africa, on May 5, 2010.

DISASTER

On June 9 the winds picked up again. They gusted even higher the next day, reaching 70 miles (113 km) per hour. The winds caused 30-foot (9-m) waves to slam into the boat. Abby attempted to restart the wet engine, but it didn't respond.

Abby knew she needed to talk to her parents about what to do. Her call home disconnected after a few minutes. Her parents waited for her to call back, but the call never came.

A sudden gust tossed Abby down the starboard bulkhead into the galley, or kitchen area, of the sailboat. She hit her head on a metal gauge, which knocked her unconscious.

When Abby woke up, she realized that she was sitting on the floor. Loose tools, a teakettle, and anything that wasn't tied down had tumbled on top of her. Abby felt like she was rolling, then

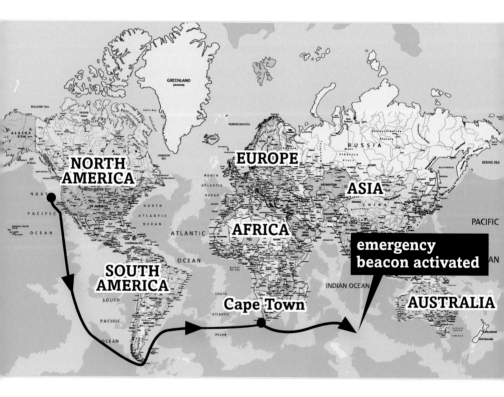

suddenly the roll stopped. *Wild Eyes* was still upright. Abby's head hurt, and everything was fuzzy. *Keep calm!* she told herself. *Act.*

Wild Eyes rocked and rolled in the waves. Abby saw that the mast had fallen. Ropes were strewn across the deck. She had to cut through them. The mast had broken and fallen beneath the boat. If it shifted, it could poke a hole in the hull and sink the boat. Abby was devastated. She knew she was in real trouble.

It was time to call home. Abby went below deck. Water covered the cabin floor. Everything, including the phones, was soaked. Both phones were dead.

Abby tried to fix them and whispered a prayer, but the phones refused to work. The trip was over. The only goal now was survival. Abby was in the middle of the Indian Ocean, hundreds of miles from help.

CALLING FOR HELP

Abby used her only option, the emergency beacons called EPIRBs, to call for help. One hung on the nearby wall. She took it down and pulled the switch. A white light pulsed in her face. She said later, "Flipping that switch was the hardest thing I ever had to do." It meant the end of her trip and the end of her dream.

ANXIOUS MOMENTS

In California, Abby's parents waited for her to call back. The longer they waited, the more worried they became.

The phone finally rang at 4:45 in the morning on June 10. It was the Coast Guard Center in Alameda, California, reporting that an emergency beacon had been activated on *Wild Eyes*. The U.S. Coast Guard had alerted the Coast Guard in Australia and on Réunion Island to begin a search-and-rescue operation.

Meanwhile, Abby remembered that she also had a MicroPLB, a personal locator beacon. Pushing it would indicate that the EPIRB didn't go off by accident, which sometimes happens. It would let rescuers know she sent the message on purpose.

COLD AND IN PAIN

Abby, soaking wet and cold, made her way to the forward sail compartment where she stored her clothing, food, and other supplies. She was relieved to find the compartment dry. Now that the storm had calmed, she changed into dry clothes and pulled out a spare sleeping bag and pillow. She crawled into the sleeping bag, but worry kept her awake. She did warm up, though, and that's when pain set in. Her leg was swollen and bruised, her head throbbed, and her right foot hurt badly. When she touched it, it was wet. Apparently, she had cut it as she scrambled around on deck. She found a T-shirt and used it to stop the bleeding before finally falling asleep.

SEARCHING FOR ABBY

While Abby was sleeping, Michael Wear, a member of the Western Water Police, a branch of the Western Australian Police Force, received a call about a distress signal from Abby Sunderland. He wanted to know where the call had originated.

"From the center of the Indian Ocean," his colleague John Fornell told him. He added that Australian Maritime Safety had chartered a Qantas Airbus to aid in the search.

The plane took off from Perth with a dozen volunteers from the State Emergency Services on board. The volunteers would act as spotters, trying to see *Wild Eyes* from the air.

Abby's boat was spotted by rescuers from the air.

SPOTTING ABBY

The Qantas plane left Perth at 7:40 a.m. and flew five and a half hours to the location indicated by the emergency beacons. The plane dipped to 1,500 feet (460 m). Whitecaps dotted the choppy sea. Rescuers feared it would be impossible to find one small sailboat in the midst of such rough water. Rescuers didn't know if the boat was upright or not. But Abby had painted a giant red heart on the bottom of her boat in case she capsized.

Abby's team of rescuers delivered her to safety.

Suddenly one of the spotters yelled that they saw her.

Everyone cheered. The boat was upright.

John Carr, the Qantas pilot, turned on his radio. "*Wild Eyes, Wild Eyes*, this is Qantas Rescue Flight, how do you hear me?"

ON THE BOAT

Abby raced below and flipped on her radio. "This is *Wild Eyes*," she said.

The plane circled for nearly two hours. The pilot reassured Abby that help was on the way. A rescue ship would reach her in about 24 hours. Australian Water Rescue called Abby's family with the good news.

As the French fishing boat, *Ile de la Réunion*, chugged toward Abby, the Qantas plane flew overhead, guiding the fishing boat.

Abby called home from the French boat to assure her parents that she was fine. She was sorry to leave *Wild Eyes* drifting in the ocean, but there was no easy way to get the damaged boat back to land.

On June 26 the fishing boat reached Réunion Island. The world celebrated Abby's safe return. A few days later, Abby was home in California. She wrote a book about her adventure, *Unsinkable: A Young Woman's Courageous Battle on the High Seas*.

On December 31, 2018, a plane spotted *Wild Eyes* floating, capsized and covered with barnacles, off Kangaroo Island, Australia.

GLOSSARY

aquatic—living or growing in water

autopilot—a mechanical or electrical system that guides the boat without help from a person

bow—the forward end of a vessel

helm—the tiller or wheel used to steer a boat

hypothermia—a life-threatening condition that occurs when a person's body temperature falls several degrees below normal

list—to tip to one side

marine biologist—a scientist who studies ocean life

mast—a rigid, vertical pole that supports the sails on a boat

Mayday—an international distress signal used by ships and planes

port—the left-hand side of a vessel, facing forward; also, a harbor in a city where boats can dock and unload

ration—to limit to prevent running out of something

rigging—the structure on a sailboat that supports the sails, including the mast and the stays or supports that keep it from blowing over

SOS—an internationally recognized signal of distress sent in radio code

starboard—the right-hand side of a vessel, facing forward

stern—the rear part of a vessel

triggerfish—a fish that lives in tropical waters and has a large dorsal spine

zoology—the branch of science dealing with animals

READ MORE

Olson, Tod. *Lost in the Pacific, 1942: Not a Drop to Drink*. New York: Scholastic Inc., 2016.

Skrypuch, Marsha Forchuk. *Adrift at Sea: A Vietnamese Boy's Story of Survival*. Toronto, Ontario, Canada: Pajama Press Inc., 2016.

Temple, Bob. *The Titanic: An Interactive History Adventure*. North Mankato, MN: Capstone Press, 2016.

Tougias, Michael, and Casey Sherman. *The Finest Hours: The True Story of a Heroic Sea Rescue*. New York: Christy Ottaviano Books/ Henry Holt and Company, 2014.

INTERNET SITES

Abby Sunderland's Blog
http://soloround.blogspot.com

National Geographic Book Talk: The Last Man Off
https://news.nationalgeographic.com/2015/05/150520-antarctica-fishing-patagonian-toothfish-albatross-oceans-ngbooktalk/

William A. Butler's Stories
http://www.wbutler.com/Stories/index.html

SOURCE NOTES

p. 6, "It was the kind of night…" Andrew Wilson. *Shadow of the Titanic: The Extraordinary Stories of Those Who Survived*. New York: Atria, 2011, p. 25.

p. 8, "Men and women were running…" Mac Smith. *Mainers on the* Titanic. Camden, Maine: Down East Books, 2014, p. 81.

p. 8, "We had no idea the boat would sink," *Shadow of the Titanic*, p. 42.

p. 10, "Even then we thought…" Jack Thayer. *Jack Thayer and the Wreck of the Titanic: Educational Version*. Learning Island.com, 2013, p. 14.

p. 11, "We were a mass of hopeless…" "Forgotten Journal Reveals How Man Survived 1912 Disaster," *New York Post*, August 8, 2012, https://nypost.com/2012/04/08/forgotten-journal-reveals-how-man-survived-1912-disaster/ Accessed on March 21, 2019.

p. 11, "In a minute" *Jack Thayer and the Wreck…* p. 16.

p. 22, "I hope no one will ever have to break that record" Tijana Radeska, "Poon Lim – The Man Who Survived 133 Days at Sea on a Wooden Raft," *Vintage News*, Sept. 14, 2016, www.thevintagenews.com/2016/09/14/poon-lim-man-survived-133-days-sea-wooden-raft Accessed on March 21, 2019.

p. 24, "We found ourselves surrounded…" Monica Rhor, "Couple Home After Sea Ordeal; Family, Friends Greet Miami Residents Who Spent 66 Days in a Life Raft," *Sun Sentinel*, August 27, 1989, https://www.sun-sentinel.com/news/fl-xpm-1989-08-27-8902280023-story.html Accessed on March 21, 2019.

p. 25, "We grabbed a lot of things…" Ibid.

p. 26, "The first two weeks…" "66 Days Fighting to Stay Alive; Couple Caught Fish, Played Mind Games on Life Raft," *Orlando Sentinel*, August 22, 1989, http://odinproxy010.odin.nodak.edu/login?url=https://search.proquest.com/docview/277541700?accountid=44562 Accessed on March 21, 2019.

p. 27, "Our family was our reason to survive" "Couple Home After Sea Ordeal…"

p. 29, "We're sinking!" William Butler, *66 Days Adrift* excerpt, http://www.wbutler.com/Stories/AAAE%20A%20SCENE%20FROM%2066%20DAYS%20ADRIFT.htm Accessed on March 21, 2019.

p. 30, "We were so overjoyed…" Barry Bearak, "Couple's Boat Sunk by Whales: Pacific 'Unfriendly,' Man Says After 66 Days on Raft," *Los Angeles Times*, August 22, 1989, http://articles.latimes.com/1989-08-22/news/mn-912_1_whale-attacks Accessed on March 21, 2019.

p. 30, "I like being on land…" "Couple Home After Sea Ordeal…"

p. 31, "I do believe a sperm whale…" Rebecca Coxon, "The Real Moby Dick: Do Whales Really Attack Humans?" BBC News, December 20, 2013, https://www.bbc.com/news/science-environment-25430996 Accessed on March 21, 2019.

p. 31, "or one of their own…" "66 Days Fighting to Stay Alive…"

p. 39, "What's happening?" Matt Lewis. *Last Man Off: A True Story of Disaster and Survival on the Antarctic Seas*. New York: Plume, 2014, p. 100.

p. 41, "Just jump…" Ibid., p. 114.

p. 41, "Come on!" Ibid., p. 113.

p. 42, "I wasn't scared…" Ibid., p. 100.

p. 44, "There's a light!" Ibid., p. 160.

p. 46, "For me, a day on the water…" Abby Sunderland. *Unsinkable: A Young Woman's Courageous Battle on the High Seas*. Nashville: Thomas Nelson, 2011, p. 15.

p. 48, "Some days…" Ibid., p. 90.

p. 55, "Flipping that switch…" Ibid., p. 158.

p. 57, "From the center of the Indian Ocean…" Ibid., p. 169.

p. 59, "*Wild Eyes, Wild Eyes*…" Ibid., p. 178.

p. 59, "This is *Wild Eyes*…" Ibid., p. 179.

SELECT BIBLIOGRAPHY

Books

Lewis, Matt. *Last Man Off: A True Story of Disaster and Survival on the Antarctic Seas.* New York: Plume, 2014.

Smith, Mac. *Mainers on the* Titanic. Camden, Maine: Down East Books, 2014.

Sunderland, Abby. *Unsinkable: A Young Woman's Courageous Battle on the High Seas.* Nashville: Thomas Nelson, 2011.

Wilson, Andrew. *Shadow of the Titanic: The Extraordinary Stories of Those Who Survived.* New York: Atria, 2011.

Websites and Articles

"66 Days Fighting to Stay Alive; Couple Caught Fish, Played Mind Games on Life Raft," *Orlando Sentinel*, August 22, 1989, http://odinproxy010.odin.nodak.edu/login?url=https://search.proquest.com/docview/277541700?accountid=44562 Accessed on March 21, 2019.

Bearak, Barry, "Couple's Boat Sunk by Whales: Pacific 'Unfriendly,' Man Says After 66 Days on Raft," *Los Angeles Times*, August 22, 1989, http://articles.latimes.com/1989-08-22/news/mn-912_1_whale-attacks Accessed on March 21, 2019.

Burke, Owen James, "*Last Man Off*: Author and Shipwreck Survivor Matt Lewis Discusses Disaster, Survival and Regret in the Southern Ocean," *The Scuttlefish*, September 18, 2015, http://thescuttlefish.com/2015/09/last-man-off-author-and-shipwreck-survivor-matt-lewis-discusses-disaster-survival-and-regret-in-the-southern-ocean/ Accessed on March 21, 2019.

Butler, William A., *William A. Butler, Adventurer, Author of 66 Days Adrift*, 2011, www.wbutler.com/ Accessed on March 21, 2019.

"Forgotten Journal Reveals How Man Survived 1912 Disaster," *New York Post*, August 8, 2012, https://nypost.com/2012/04/08/forgotten-journal-reveals-how-man-survived-1912-disaster/ Accessed on March 21, 2019.

Harnett, Richard M., "Chinese Only Survivor of U-Boat Attack: Book Recounts 133-Day Ordeal on Raft," *Los Angeles Times*, December 8, 1985, http://articles.latimes.com/print/1985-12-08/local/me-14954_1_raft Accessed on March 21, 2019.

Hartog, Kelly, "Solo-Sail Girl's Miracle at Sea – 16-year-old Feared Lost at Sea Is Found Alive in Indian Ocean," *New York Post*, June 11, 2010; p. 6.

Lennon, Troy, "Sole Survivor of the Sinking of the *Ben Lomond* in WWII, Poon Lim, Set a Record for 133 Days Adrift at Sea," *The Daily Telegraph*, Apr. 2018 [Sydney, Australia], https://www.dailytelegraph.com.au/news/sole-survivor-of-the-sinking-of-the-benlomond-in-wwii-poon-lim-set-a-record-for-133-days-adrift-at-sea/news-story/9c63348c42762182e17bcc3c2ddbe1a8 Accessed on March 21, 2019.

Lunau, Kate, "Going Overboard," *MacLean's*, June 28, 2010 (vol. 123, Issue 24); p. 47-48.

"Poon Lim: Record Holder For Longest Time Spent Adrift at Sea," Adventures & Travel https://www.inaraft.com/blog/a-remarkable-story-of-survival-at-sea-poon-lim/ Accessed on March 21, 2019.

Radeska, Tijana, "Poon Lim – The Man Who Survived 133 Days at Sea on a Wooden Raft," *The Vintage News*, September 14, 2016, https://www.thevintagenews.com/2016/09/14/poon-lim-man-survived-133-days-sea-wooden-raft/ Accessed on March 21, 2019.

Rhor, Monica, "Couple Home After Sea Ordeal; Family, Friends Greet Miami Residents Who Spent 66 Days in a Life Raft," *Sun Sentinel*, August 27, 1989, https://www.sun-sentinel.com/news/fl-xpm-1989-08-27-8902280023-story.html Accessed on March 21, 2019.

Sailant, Catherine, "Solo Teen Sailor Found Safe; Australian Air Spotters Make Contact with Abby Sunderland Aboard her Boat," *Los Angeles Times*, June 11, 2010; p. AA1.

Sunderland, Abby, "Sailin' Away," *Girls' Life*, June/July 2010 (Vol. 16, Issue 6); p. 84-95.

Thayer, Jack, *Jack Thayer and the Wreck of the Titanic: Educational Version*, Learning Island.com, 2013.

Worral, Simon, "Life, Then Death, on a Trawler in Freezing Antarctic Seas," *National Geographic*, March 20, 2015, https://news.nationalgeographic.com/2015/05/150520-antarctica-fishing-patagonian-toothfish-albatross-oceans-ngbooktalk/ Accessed on March 21, 2019.

INDEX

ABOUT THE AUTHOR

Elizabeth Raum is the author of numerous books for young readers. She especially enjoys writing about people who face life-threatening challenges with courage and quick thinking. To learn more, visit her website at www.elizabethraumbooks.com.